AF316148

STECK-VAUGHN

California Gateways

Decodable Reader

Program Authors

Action Learning Systems, Inc.

Robin Scarcella, Ph.D., Hector Rivera, Ph.D., and Mabel Rivera, Ph.D.
English Language Development

Isabel L. Beck, Ph.D. and Margaret McKeown, Ph.D.
Vocabulary

Penny Chiappe-Collins, Ph.D.
Decoding, African American Vernacular English

Mastering the California Standards
Reading • Writing • Listening • Speaking

Steck Vaughn™

An Imprint of HMH
Supplemental Publishers Inc.

www.Steck-Vaughn.com
1-800-531-5015

ISBN-13: 978-1-4190-5117-3
ISBN-10: 1-4190-5117-2

1A 2 3 4 5 6 7 8 073 14 13 12 11 10 09 08

"Reading is to the mind what exercise is to the body."
—Joseph Addison

Table of Contents

{UNIT 2}

{ UNIT 4 }

Chapter 1

Chapter 2

Chapter 3

Sam's Mat

Sam sat at the mat.
Sam said, "Mat."
Sam sat and sat.

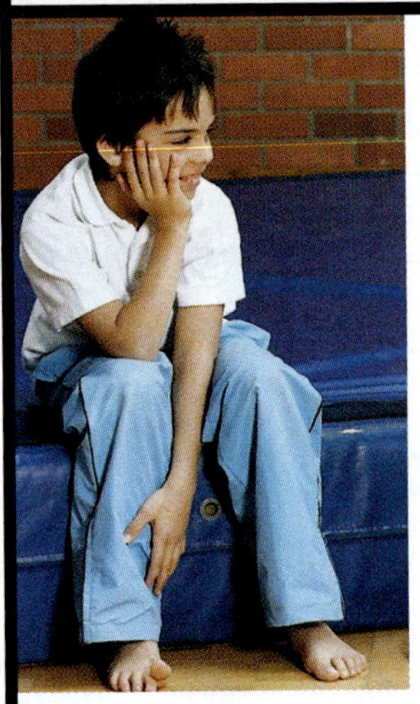

In the Ring

Tam sat.

"I am at the mat," said Tam at Sam.

Sam sat.

Tam and Sam sat at the mats.

The Hat

Tim Hin has a hat. It is tan.
It is hip.
Tim tips his hat at Pam.
"Make a hat for me!" said Pam.

Min in the Pit

Min sits in his pit.
"Pip, come in!" Min said.
Pip and Min sit in the pit.

The Shop

Pam, Pip, and Pat make hats, mats, pins, and maps.
Pip hits pins into his map.
Pam pats the mats and hats.
Pat has his nap!

Ham in a Pan

Sam has ham in a pan.
It is his ham.
Sam splits his ham with Pat,
Tim, Min, and Pam.

The Cod

Bob has a cod!
Bob pats his cod.
"Look at his cod!" Dot said.
"Pop it in the hot pot, Bob!" she said.

Dinner for Doc and Dan

Doc sits.
He nips at corn cobs.
Dan sits and nips at ham.
Doc has cobs and Dan has ham.

The Pug Dog

Huck is a pug dog.
Huck dug a big pit.
"Look at the pit Huck dug," said Rick.
"Bad dog!"

Huck and the Tick

A tick bit Huck!
Huck got sick.
"A bug is on you, Huck!" said Gus.
Rip!
Gus got the tick.

Rock in My Sock

"A rock is in my sock," said Mick.
Mick dug in his sock.
Mick dug and dug.
Mick got the rock.

Rob's Rug

Rob has a big, red rug.
Cat came and sat on his big, red rug.
A rat came and sat on his big, red rug.
"Ick!" said Rob.

Jen and Fin

Fin has a pal. Jen is his pal.
Jen has a blue pen. Fin has two.
Fin has a red bag. Jen has two.
Jen has a blue play hut. Jen let
Fin play in it. Jen and Fin are pals!

Jim the Duck

Jim is a little duck. Jim is fit.
Jim can jump. Jump, Jim, jump.
Jim can jig. Jig, Jim, jig.
Jim can run. Run, Jim, run.
Jim can play. Play, Jim, play.
Jim is a fun duck.

One Funny Dog

Wes is my pet. Wes is three. Wes is one funny dog.

My chum Wes is sick. Wes has a red dot.

Zack is his vet. Zack can check Wes. Zack can help Wes.

Wes is not sick!

Help Zeb

"Help!" Zeb calls. Zeb is in a jam in his web.

"I can help, Zeb!" Zap! Kam zaps down to Zeb.

"I can help, Zeb!" Zip! Chip zips up to Zeb.

Kam and Chip help Zeb. Zeb hugs Kam. Zeb hugs Chip.

The Big, Fat Bug

Jan saw a big, fat bug.

"Chaz, that big, fat bug is all black!"

"Get back, Jan! I bet the big, fat bug ate my cat Kal."

Jan ran. Chaz ran. Chaz saw Kal.

"Wait! Here is Kal. Kal is back!"

Jan and Chaz pet Kal.

Ken and Fez

Is Ken here? Is Fez here?
Ken is not. Fez is not.
Is Ken in a yellow wig? Is Fez
in a black hat?
It is Ken and Fez!

A Box to Fix the Van

Quick! Get a box! Lex must not quit.
Can we win if Lex can fix his van?
Yes! Did Lex get a box?
Yes, he got a box.
Did Lex fix his van?
Yes, his van is ready.
Yes! We won!

The Quiz

Max has a quiz for Viv.

Is wax made in a vat? Can a yak quack like a duck? Do you like Tex Mex dip on chips? Can a fox fit in a tux?

Good luck on his quiz, Viv!

Songs

Ding, ding, dong! The bells sing a song. This song is old.

When Mom was a kid, she sung this song. She sings lots of songs.

Ding, ding, dong! When we sing new songs, I can sing along. Ding, ding, dong!

New Fish

Josh and his pal Chang wish to get new fish. Josh must dash to a shop for fish. When can Josh take a break?

Now Josh has Math. Then Josh is in a show.

When will Josh get new fish?

Beth's Pals

Beth has six pals. Shel, Thad, Val, Jax, Max, and Ming are her pals. Shel has a brown shed. Thad runs a quick dash. Val is a math whiz. Jax likes to eat yams. Max has big cats. Ming has red fish.

The Shack

Thud! Thud! Thud!

What is that?

A shack fell.

Our shack?

Yes, our red shack!

It is thick! Why did it fall?

Josh, that brown fox is under the shack!

Quick, get it out! Rush it to a vet, please.

What's Inside?

"What is in his bag?" said Mack to Jack.
"So, is it fans? Is it cans? Is it stamps?
Is it ramps? Will it crack? Can it stack?"
"It is a pretty lamp!" said Dan.

Going Camping

Pack that backpack. Pack it up!

Put on a tag. Pack stamps. Pack pans. Pack fans. Pack sacks. Pack rags.

Put that big backpack on his ramp. Put it in his van. Soon we will ride up to camp.

How Will They Get Back?

How will Bill Swift and Jill Twig get back? Bill Swift will zip under a wall.

Then Bill will zip up a big hill. Jill Twig will slip down a tan ramp in a sack.

Then they will be back!

Drill and Fill

Can Jill drill this twig?
This is how Jill drills. Zip. Zip. Zip.
The twig chips. Good job, Jill!
Jill will stop that drill.
Can Bill fill that bin?
This is how Bill fills. Drip. Drip. Drip.
Stop, Bill! Bill spills. Bill will mop it up.

Stan Is Not Well

Where is Stan? Did Stan slip on a twig? Did Stan sit on a tack? Did Stan crack his back? Did Stan get a cramp?

"Stan is not well," said Jan.

"Yes," said Mack. "Stan is ill. He got in bed."

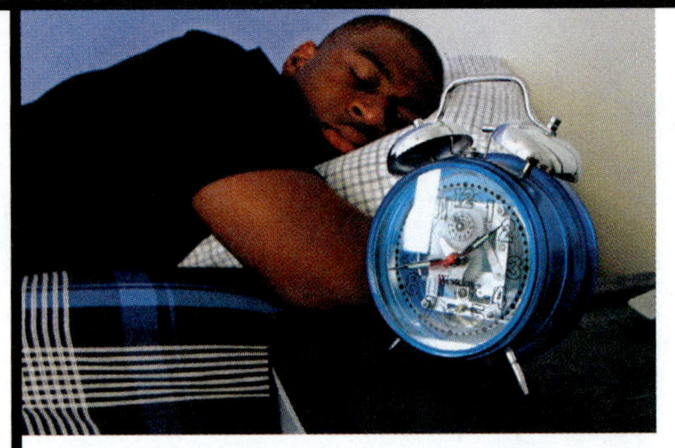

Pip Zips

Will has a cat Pip. Pip is white.
Pip has a tan spot, too.
Pip can zip there and back.
Pip will nap in his sack.
Pip will tip that lamp.
Pip will spill that milk.
Pip is a scamp!

At the Pond

"It is hot, hot, hot!" say Dot and Tom.

"Can you drop us at that pond?" ask Dot and Tom.

A flock of ducks is at that pond. Dot is fond of them. They fly, then flop.

Tom plops in. Tom is not hot!

Dot plops in. Dot is not hot!

Time for Bed

"Look at that clock. It is after ten!" say Mom and Pop.

"We do not want to stop. We will stop when a block drops!"

"Tic, tock. Tic, tock!" said Pop.

Tom props a block on top. Plop! Ten blocks drop!

Dot flops in bed. Tom flops in bed.

The Rent

"When will Trent get the rent?"
said Dad. "Trent must get it from us."

"Well," said Mom, "I just went
and hit his bell, but Trent was not in.
Trent was out on a run."

"Trent trusts us. It is not spent.
Give it to him at ten."

The Tents

Nell put up her tent. Ken put up his tent.

Then a gust blew in.

Crack! The tents bent.

Smack! The tents fell.

"We must put them up well," said Nell.

Nell put up her tent well. Ken put up his tent well.

"I trust the tents now!" said Ken.

The Gift

"What is in that big, red box?" said Dot.

"I am giving it to you. I can not tell!" said Kent.

"Is it locks? Is it clocks? Is it blocks?"

"It is not locks, clocks, or blocks. Just open it, Dot!"

"A bell! Fun! I am fond of it!"

The Well

Kell and Mom went for a quick run. They saw a big well by the pond. It had rust. It had cracks. It had a bad smell.

"Stop. Stop at that well. I think I must wish."

Kell spun. Kell put ten cents in. *Plop!*

"Tell your wish," said Mom.

"Just to have fun at the prom!" said Kell.

A Trip to the Store

"Is the trade store open, Hope?" asked Gabe.

"Yes. It is open."

"Take a coat before you go!" said Fay. "What will you get, Hope?"

"Lace to make an apron, and a loaf to make toast."

"I will get rope to stop the boat," said Gabe. "It will float away on a lake!"

"Can you get sugar, Gabe?" asked Fay. "I will make a cake when you get home!"

The Red Oak

There is a red oak in the woods. We live close, so we can walk on a road to this red oak each day. This red oak is home to a toad, a mole, and a bee.

Jake the toad has a spot on his nose. Kay the mole made a cave of stones. Joan the bee made an oval hive on the red oak.

Jake, Kay, and Joan love this red oak.

We Like to Read

Mike, Sue, Lea, and Dean will each read a book. Then Dan will give them a treat. Dan may make a pie, ice cream, or a cup of tea. He may give them five rides on a slide or more music time. He may give them a fun blue kite. A new book may even be a prize.

Thanks, Dan! We like to read!

Camping

Nine fine pines sway in the wind. Five fish dive in the lake.

Jude and Spike go on a hike over a peak. They tie the tent with twine. It has a leak.

They make a fire. They eat a huge pie. They try to be neat and clean.

Then they hear a sound.

"Who is there?"

It is just a leaf!

On the Farm

Shane has a huge farm. He takes care of a cute mule. Mules do not bite.

Cole rides a mule around the farm. He will put hay on the vines so they will grow.

Shane and Cole eat ripe grapes, a meat pie, and a round cake. When each day is over, they walk home on the road.

Gale's Birthday

It is Gale's birthday. She is nice. Jay made Gale an ice cream cake in the shape of a lime with her name on it. Jade gave Gale some pale lace. Spike made Gale a blue hat. Blake gave Gale a pet mole. Bea gave Gale a ticket to ride twice on a huge slide.

Gale thanks them again and again.

The Race

Clare fills a spare tire with air. Greer sits on a chair. The race will begin at any time.

Clare hears the start with her ears. The cars zoom away. Any car can win. The best cars will steer well and go far. Omar's car goes to the front. Blair's car appears near the rear.

Omar's car wins! He is a star! Cheer for Omar!

The Dare

Jamar has a dare to tell Barb.
Jamar dares Barb to ride a cart
down a hill at the park. They push
the green cart up the yard. The
hill at the park is all clear.

"Go! Steer, Barb! Steer!"

"Oh no!"

Crash! Barb flies through the
air. She lands *smack!*

That dare was not smart.

Yuri's Spurs

"Who made these spurs?" asked Yuri.

"Me! Those spurs are for you," said Homer. "Spurs can make you soar."

"Spurs will make me soar over floors?"

"Yes, sir. Faster than a laser can cut a door!"

"I will be swifter than a boar with fur," said Yuri. "I will roar!"

"Yuri, you will roar like a motor with those spurs."

"I am happy to have these spurs, Homer!"

Poor Kirk

Poor Kirk. He is sick. Kirk must stay indoors. He is all by himself.

He looks out a window. He spots the curb. He hears two birds that chirp. Both birds lurk near his door.

He wishes he was not indoors. He wants to soar like the birds. Poor Kirk.

A Fun Jar

"Do you have a spare jar?" asked Mark.

"Yes," said Thor. "I have a clear jar."

"Could I use it, please?"

"I will share my jar, but take care. It is rare," said Thor.

"I will not drop it on a floor or down a set of stairs."

"This jar is bare, Mark."

"Yes, but hold it to your ear, Thor. Hear the roar of a cold sea?"

"Yes, I can! What do you call this jar?"

"A fun jar!" said Mark.

The Storm

Clark spies a storm. It is almost near the barn. The swirls of cold air are as loud as a horn. The storm shakes the barn hard, but it stays firm.

Clark hopes the storm will spare the barn. It is his job to care for the animals.

A horse is hurt. She has a scar on her fur. Clark uses his torn shirt to make her warm.

The List

Joon made a list. Then she read it. It said: *Wash the fruit. Shred it. Put it in the shell. Cook.* She was fast, but she did not ruin it.

Then Joon got a call. It was Lew.

"Quick, Joon," Lew said. "What can I bring?"

"Bring cool tea," said Joon.

Soon her bell rang. It was her three pals: Lew, Brock, and Stan.

"Hello!" Joon said.

"I smell a pie," said Brock.

"Yes!" said Joon. "Pull up a seat!"

On a Cruise

"Did you bring a bathing suit? We are going on a cruise!"

Toot, toot! The horn just blew. The cruise ship zooms away.

What a thrill! Every pal is here: Stew, Brad, Willie, and Brit, to name a few.

Willie threw a hook over the side.

"Did you pull up any fish, Willie?" He shrugs.

"It is okay. Look at all this food! Have some juice. Have a cookie."

The Kite

"I wish I had a new kite," Saul said. Then he saw a string.

"I know! I can use that thread to make a kite."

Trish got Saul card stock paper. He cut a square. He put five threads on the square.

"I will fly my kite," said Saul. It did not fly. Why?

"I know!" said Saul. "I need wind for my kite to soar."

Soon a spring wind came. His kite flew.

Maud's Claw

Maud the crab got her claw stuck.

"Help!" she squeaks. "I am in a trap. It is on my vein. My claw will not spread."

She sings, "I wish I was free."

Her pal Trent hears her song. He hauls a straw to the trap.

"This trap has a flaw," says Trent.

He springs open the trap with the straw. Maud is free!

Paul

Once a girl had a bird named Paul. Paul was her best pal. Paul flew away.

The girl tried to look for Paul, but this did not work. She was sad. She could not sleep.

In the spring, she went to the town square. There, she sat down. She threw bread. A bird saw a shred by a shrub. Squawk!

It was Paul. She found her best pal Paul!

Claud the Thief

Claud was a thief. He broke into a store. First he stole a book about squids. He threw it in his sack. Then he took some string. He stole a better suit, too. His old suit shrunk.

Then he tried to sprint away. He threw his sack in a shrub to hide it.

A cop caught Claud and found the sack.

The cop said, "There is a law. You will go to jail for stealing."

The Snow

Sue saw the gray sky. It had a glow. Will snow fall? No!

Snow did fall. It blew and it blew. When Sue got home, there was snow up past her toe. Snow was up to her gate.

"No!" said Sue. "How will I dig this snow?" Then she saw a pail.

"Hold on!" Sue said. "I will bring this pail so I can dig the snow." Sue did.

It is time for Sue to play in the snow!

The Date

Things look bad for Glen and Kate. They were on a date.

Then her cute hat blew away. She tried to hold on. It hit a snag on a shrub. It flew like a sail in a breeze.

Glen tried to grab the hat, but it was too late. He saw the hat blow by in a blur.

Then the hat fell on his toe.

Kate ran at her hat. She grabbed it. She did not let it blow away again.

Fred and the Bear

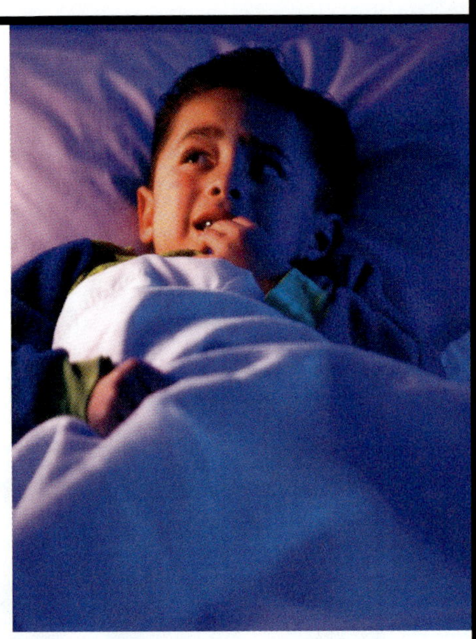

My brother Fred drew a big, wild bear. It had huge teeth.

That night Fred lay in bed. His light was off. There was a screech. What if it were a bear? What if it hurt him? What if it were to bite him?

"Hey, Sam!" Fred said. "A bear is in my bed!"

I came in.

"Do not cry. Bears live far away. That screech was the car. Dad is home!"

Dad gave Fred a hug. Then he went to bed.

What Will You Draw?

"What will you draw?" asked Skylar.

"I will draw a red and blue kite that can fly in the sky," said Fran.

"I will draw a child who is giving a speech," said Lacey.

"I will draw a key that might open a box," said Grant.

"I will draw a wild bird that can screech at night," said Riley.

"Can that bird bite?" asked Fran.

"He will bite if you try to fight him!" said Riley.

Skip and Joe

Skip and Joe go for a walk in the woods to see wild birds.

"Joe, did you bring a drink?" Skip said.

"Yes. I keep a drink with me when it is hot!"

They sat by a beech tree. Skip had a sip.

"What is this blue brew?"

"It is a fruit drink. I use peach, grape, and berry," said Joe. "Hey, Skip, we need to eat."

"You are right," said Skip. "I am glad I always carry a snack."

Wish on a Star

There is a bright yellow glow in the sky. Is it a full moon? Is it a huge kite on fire? It is moving at a quick rate. It is a shooting star!

Dan and his child see the star fly by. They grin. Dan says, "Make a wish. It is always good luck to wish on a shooting star."

The child makes three wishes. "I wish for a blue oboe, a brown snail, and a green frog to keep."

The Flower Garden

Mike and Marcus went to a flower shop. Mike got seed packets. Marcus got a rake. Then they went home to start a garden. Mike dug holes for the seeds.

"Open a packet," said Mike.

Marcus put seeds in the dirt. Mike got a hose.

"We will give them water," said Mike.

"To keep them clean, Mike?"

"No! It will help them grow!" said Mike.

Pop's Big Day

"Today is a big day for Pop," said Mike.

"We can get him a gift at a store," said Marcus.

"Okay!" said Mike. "We can go to a bookstore."

Mike and Marcus went to the corner bookstore. Then they went upstairs.

"Pop likes this kind of book," said Marcus.

"Pick a long book!" said Mike.

Mike and Marcus got Pop a long book and a card. The bookstore lady said the book was a thriller!

The Spaceship

Last night Ellie and Richard took a stroll. They saw a glow on a path. It was a silver ball. It was much too dark to see it well.

Richard got his flashlight. Then they saw a spaceship!

"I do not believe it!" said Ellie.

"I do not believe it myself!" said Richard. "Can you see in it?"

Ellie took a look. It had green man in it!

"*Snopit*! *Skaydug*!" the spaceman said.

The Spaceman

Ellie and Richard found a silver spaceship. It had a green man in it.

"*Blowbate, Zoopdeer Zapfrog zeermag boamair*!" he said.

"What did you say?" Ellie said.

"I shall say it in a new way," the spaceman said. "Hello, I am Zoopdeer Zapfrog. I am a spaceman. I mean no harm."

"Hey!" Richard said. "How did you say that?"

"I have been here five times!" Zoopdeer Zapfrog said.

The Hike

"Pack up all backpacks! It is time to begin," said Taylor. She was the leader.

The campers began to hike.

"Stay together," said Taylor. "Try to keep up."

"Doowop, diddy, diddy," sang the campers. It made the hike go faster.

At last the campers saw a lake. It was nearly nighttime.

"We will make camp on this spot," said Taylor. "I will show you how to put up a tent."

The Campers

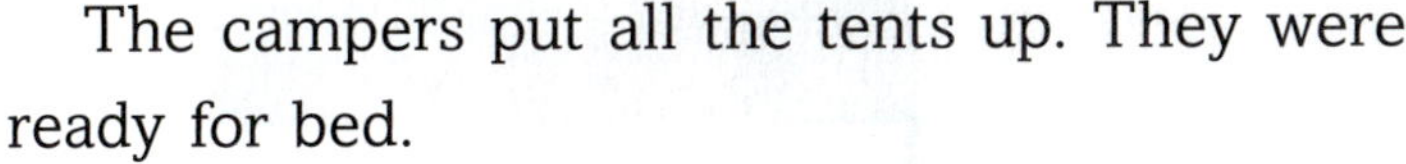

The campers put all the tents up. They were ready for bed.

"Never put food out!" said Taylor. "Keep it all in this cooler."

All campers went to sleep. Then they woke up. There was a roar!

"Oh, no!" said Ned. "I forgot a candy bar!"

Ned ran to the tent flap. He saw a big beast.

"Castons! Bugbay . . . bairdig! Ronit . . . riferan!" Ned said. "I mean, 'Campers! Bear! Run!'"

To a Parade

A boy had on a pumpkin costume. He was on his way to a parade.

He got stuck in the front door. He was too wide! So he rang the doorbell. His mom came to the door.

"Look, Mom!" he said. "I am stuck! I did not think this would happen!"

"I will unzip it. Then you can get back in it outside!"

The Surprise

Mindy found a letter in her bag. It said, "Follow these steps and you will get a treat! Take fifteen steps west. Then follow the stone path. Step into the park. Look only under a blanket with red checks."

Mindy saw her treat. It was a picnic basket. Then her sister Nancy said, "Surprise! Take a napkin, Mindy. Let's eat! It is still warm."

"This was a good surprise," said Mindy. "I'm hungry!"

Lunchtime!

April and Ira made their own lunch. They put on aprons. Then they got out the bread.

"What will it be today?" asked Ira.

"Tuna and mayo for me!" said April.

"Lunchmeat for me!" said Ira. "So, let's go for it! Do you want tomato?"

"Yes, I would like a small slice," said April.

Lunch was made. They each had an apple on the side. It was good.

My Buddy

I have a buddy. He likes to follow me.

Sometimes he is long and dark. Other times he is small and wide.

This buddy likes to play. He also likes sunlight. He will go away when it is very dark.

Maybe we will see him today. Maybe we will not. If it is sunny, we will see him.

Do you know who my buddy is? He is my shadow!

Sounds from a Bush

Katie was on her way to soccer practice.

A *chirp chirp* came from a bush.

Katie saw a baby bird. Then she saw a nest. It was broken on the sidewalk.

"I will get help," she said. Katie went to tell her mom.

They called a vet so they would know what to do. They came back with a box.

"Open the box," said Mom. "Let me pick it up. We will take it to a person who can care for it."

The Big Game

Tammy and her brother Teddy were on the same baseball team. Tammy was a pitcher. Teddy was a catcher.

Tonight was a big game. It was against the Yankees. Teddy had a plan.

"At the start of the game, just throw your fastball. In the second inning, we will surprise them with curveballs."

"I like it," said Tammy. "I hope I can throw on target!"

Your Birthday

Smile! It is your birthday!

Make a wish. Then we can have cake and punch. The cups, plates, and spoons match the punch.

I will pinch you seven times for luck.

Mom will take a bunch of photos.

I got a gift that took a long time to wrap. It is a photo album that you can write phrases in. I hope that you like it.

This is a gift from Dad. It is a baseball that you can pitch and catch.

Your birthday will be tons of fun!

A Weird Day

My phone rang today. A man said, "Is Finch there?"

"No, there is no Finch here. You might have the wrong number," I said. "Have a nice day!"

Then I went to eat lunch with a pal. I got an itch, so I stood up to scratch. At the same time, my arm hit a man.

"Oh no!" I said. "I did not mean to do that."

"It is okay," he said. "Nothing is wrong. My name is Finch."

"Is he the same Finch from the phone?" I thought.

What a weird day!

A Twinge for Fudge

Vince had a twinge for fudge. He took a glance in the fridge. No fudge.

He went out his door and shut the fence gate. He got into his car and drove over a bridge.

He took a glance back at a boat stuck in sludge. He drove his car by the school and the lodge, near the edge of town.

Then he got to a house. He went under a hedge and up to the door.

"Mrs. Brown, may I please have some fudge? Your fudge is the best!"

At the Winter Ball

Prince Lance is at a ball. He sits on the edge of his chair and plays with its fringe. He will not budge.

Prince Lance is shy. He has a scheme to not dance.

Then, Madge glances at him.

"I am Madge," she says. "Is there a chance that you might dance with me?"

"I can not dance," says Prince Lance. "I have two left feet."

"I will not judge your dance skill," says Madge.

"Okay. I will dance with you."

Prince Lance lunges onto the dance floor. He and Madge dance together all night long.

The Dry Farm

Crunch, crunch, crunch.

Spence walks over the hard ground. It has not rained since last month. Not even an inch. The ground is dry. The flower patch has dried up, so he put phony flowers in a hedge.

A hinge on the fence squeaks. It is too dry.

Spence glances at the sky. A drop plops on his head. It makes him flinch.

Then rain falls down in buckets. It is like the sky has wrung a sponge over the farm. Now the farm has a chance to grow.

Phil's Tale

Phil likes to write. He wrote a fun tale. It is about a badger and a hedgehog that live under a bench. They are pals.

One day they look for a new home. They look at a ledge in a ditch. They look at a patch near the school. They look at a fence on a ranch. They look at a whole range of homes.

Then the badger said, "There is nothing wrong with our old home."

"You are right," said the hedgehog. "We will go back to our bench. It is home."

A Chicken That Oinks

When Father was a boy, he had a pet chicken. This pet was loyal to him. It would follow him to school each day. His chicken did not cluck. It would oink! What a silly noise for a chicken to make!

His chicken ate a lot of soy. It had a foil toy that it did enjoy. Then one day, this foil toy got lost. Some other boys did join Father to look for the foil toy. They did not even avoid looking in an oil well. They never found it. His chicken never did oink again.

A Game of Royals

Joy had a doll in her bedroom. It sat upon a doily. Joy forgot she had the old toy. One day, it came to life. It said, "I am a real doll! I will play a fun game."

"Join me," the doll begged the other toys. "Try not to make too much noise. I hope Joy will not hear us.

"This game is 'Royals.' When you throw a coin, you get points. One point for heads and two points for tails. The toy that has the most points wins!"

A Monster House

There is a house in town with a brown door. The door looks like a mouth. The windows look like eyes. Trees around this house look like feet and hands. At night children from town sneak out to this house. They say that a monster once got stuck inside. Now they say they hear this monster howl at night.

One night a man heard a loud creak. The next day he found a couch on the lawn.

No one saw who put it on the lawn. The children say the monster inside the house spit it out.

A Crowd of Clouds

Howie and Chou sat down at the playground.

"Look at that crowd of clouds," said Chou. He pointed to one with his hand.

"That cloud looks like a cow, or maybe it is a hound. *Bow-wow!*"

"Now it looks like a clown with big feet," said Howie. "It has a crown and a frown."

Then a swift wind blew in. The clouds blew round and round. A black cloud came by. It made a loud sound.

"Wow!" said Howie. "We must go home before the rain starts to pound!"

"We can watch the clouds from our couch!" said Chou.

Captain Oily Oyster

"Ahoy!" says Captain Oily Oyster. He spots a cloud.

"Hoist the sails, boys! Get out of port now! I want to avoid this storm. I do not enjoy storms!"

The name of his ship is the *Royal Duck*. It smells foul. Many men toil to hoist the huge sails. They are loyal to their captain.

There is a loud noise. Oily Oyster frowns. "Ahoy! What is that sound?"

Then he spies a flash of lightning in the dark sky. The storm is near. He cries, "Hold on, boys! I vow that we will not drown!"

Pigs in the Garden

I think I hear a noise. I stick my head out my window to look. It sounds like an *oink*. I see soil fly out of our garden.

"Mom, come quick!" I say. "There are pigs in our garden!" They are spoiling her flowers.

Mom takes a coat and runs to our garden. There is a big void where her flowers were. Her blood starts to boil. Her face grows red as she scowls. She grabs a plow and runs at the pigs. "Scram!" she cries.

"*Oink, oink, oink,*" the pigs reply. They like our garden. They want to stay.

Fresh Corn

"Turn off here. I see a sign!" Jonah shouts.

Mom steers to the right. We drive over a big hill.

At the top, we see miles and miles of corn fields. We drive past a huge gnome with a sign that says: "Corn Farm."

It took us an hour to get here. We came here to pick our own corn!

Jonah gives Mom a look. He swats a gnat and asks, "What is wrong with corn from a store?"

Mom grew up on a farm. She knows that fresh corn is the best.

Sara the Designer

When she grows up, Sara plans to design clothes. She likes to make things. That is why she would like to be a designer.

She has the honor of asking a designer questions at a fashion show.

Sara: "What is this girl in?"

Designer: "She has on our ghost skirt."

Sara: "How did you make the fire design?"

Designer: "I cut out red swirls. Then I had to stitch them on."

Sara loves the white skirt. She draws a sketch of a skirt she would like to make.

She hopes to be a top designer!

Did You Know?

My brother John got a new book, *Animal Facts That Will Wow Your Pals.*

He knocked on my door and said, "Did you know that a fish egg does not have a shell?"

"Yes, I knew that. A frog egg also has no shell."

"Did you know that pigs are not dumb?"

"Yes," I said. "Pigs are smart and clean."

"Well, did you know that wool is from lambs?"

"Yes," I said. "People comb their wool and then knit with it."

"Did you know all mammals have knees?"

"I did not," I said. "That is a good fact!"

Ned the Knight

Ned the Knight said goodbye to his family.
He left his home to fight for the king. He threw
a comb into his sack and tied it up with a knot.

Then he walked for miles. His limbs grew
numb. He knew it would be a long trip, but
he was not ready for such a long climb up the
mountain to the castle.

When he got to a door, he struck the
knocker. A knob turned and a knight took a
peek out. Ned spoke up, "I am Ned the Knight.
I am here to fight for the king!"

The Sick Lamb

Farmer Chris had a cow and a lamb that were best pals. They would play and eat grass. They would climb up a hill and then slide down.

One day the lamb got sick. Chris did not know what was wrong. He worried about his lamb. He took a look at his crops. He saw that gnats were eating the wheat stalks that his lamb ate. Those gnats had made his lamb sick.

Chris got some medicine for his lamb. When the lamb was well, it ran back to the barn to play with its pal the cow again.

Cooking with Dad

"Be very safe with that knife!" Dad shouts. "Do not chop off your thumb!"

He shows me how to align the knife with the edge of the board.

We are cooking spaghetti. I chop onions for the sauce. I gnaw on gum so that I will not cry while I chop. Dad whips the meat and cheese together in a pot. The pasta sits in a pile on a plate.

Then some meat lands on the floor.

"It was not me!" I say. "It was a ghost!"

Dad smiles, "I will keep my eye out for a hungry ghost!"

A Squirrel in the House

"Don't let that squirrel in the house!" Mom screams. I thought that I had shut our door, but it is wide open. The squirrel runs through the open door. We chase after it.

The squirrel hops on a new chair that Mom just bought. Then it runs over a rough blue rug. We chase it through the kitchen and out the back door. Mom slams the door shut.

Then the squirrel taps on the glass door with its nose. It will not go away. I thought that the squirrel would have had enough of running through our house!

Doug the Cowboy

Doug is a cowboy on the Rough and Tough Ranch. His job is to round up the cows. Each day, he rides his horse on the ranch.

Since a drought hit the ranch, dust has been swirling all over. When Doug rode through the dust, he would cough. Then he saw another cowboy with a bandana over his mouth.

"I ought to get a bandana. That should stop my cough," Doug thought.

So he bought one. Now he puts a bandana over his mouth to keep the dust out.

Gold Bars

"Did you see the morning paper yet?" asked Colt.

"Which paper?" said Walt.

"*The Daily Call.*"

"Not yet. What did it say?"

"A load of freight fell off a bridge," said Colt.

"What is the freight?"

"It is eighty-eight old gold bars."

"Wow!" Walt cried. "That must weigh a ton!"

"I bet it sunk down deep in the river."

"We should find it!"

"Good plan, Walt. Then we can wash it and take it back to the people who own it," said Colt.

"Maybe they will give us an old gold bar as a reward!"

The Sleigh Ride

Snow covers the ground. It is time for a sleigh ride! The sleigh holds eight people. Each boy and girl bought a ticket to ride on the sleigh. One by one they walk to the sleigh and jump in.

Waldo puts his hands in his pockets to keep warm. It is cold outside. As the sleigh glides through the woods, a girl calls out, "Hold on to your seat! Don't fall!"

Sleigh bells ring as the reins shake. Waldo begins to sing a winter song. Everyone else joins in. Even the horse neighs! What a fun sleigh ride!

Signs of the Seasons

The first leaf to drop is a sign that fall is near. A very cold day is a sign that winter is near. A red robin is a sign that spring is near. That means warm weather will soon be here!

What could be the first sign of summer? Should it be the first day that it hits eighty? Should it be when it stays light through eight o'clock? Or should the first sign just be June twenty-first! What would you say?

Mother's Birthday

"What should I get Mother for her birthday?" asked Holt.

"I don't know," said Edward. "I bought her a sweater."

"That is nice. I could get bath salts to calm her or a kitty she could care for."

"You should buy her a small colt."

"That would cost my weight in gold!"

"True. You could get a nice watch," said Edward.

"I know! I will give her a walking stick. Mother likes to hike. A stick would be helpful on a rough climb."

"Where are those sold?"

"I thought the outdoor store sold them."

"Great plan, Holt! Let's go!"

The Letter

JoAnn walked out to the mailbox. There was a letter inside. It was from her brother. He was on vacation on a sailboat. The name of the sailboat was *Teardrop*.

He wrote to her about his adventures at sea. He saw a starfish and some seashells. Her brother ate a lot of seafood.

He wrote that he was a bit homesick, but he liked being on the sailboat. Each day he saw the sunrise and sunset. He wrote that the red and orange sun looked like a wildfire on the sea. All that sun gave him a bad sunburn!

Snowflakes

A snowflake falls on a sidewalk. Another snowflake falls on a playground to the right of a baseball field. Then snowflakes fall in a few backyards. Soon snowflakes are falling all over town. Most people stay inside, but some kids run out to the schoolyard. They sled down a big hill. One kid has a stopwatch to time how fast the sleds go.

By nightfall the town is hidden under a white blanket of snow. Then the snowplows hit the streets. By morning there is no snow on the sidewalks and streets.

My Sister's Notebook

My sister loved to write and draw in her notebook. She never left home without it. She even brought it with her when we went camping.

When we got to the campsite, she took her notebook out of her backpack. She drew a picture of a butterfly and a bullfrog that she saw.

Then she drew a picture of a bluebird in its nest. She wrote a story about raindrops that fell on our tent.

"Sis," I said, "there is no rain!"

My sister laughed, "That is why this is fiction!"

Would You Like Some Tea?

"Would you like a cup of tea?" Marybeth asked Jackson.

"Yes, please," Jackson said. "Did you make those cupcakes?"

"Yes, they are homemade. I made the shortbread and sandwiches, too."

Marybeth poured the tea. Her teacups were buttercup yellow with a design that looked like wallpaper.

"Jackson, would you like some milk in your tea?"

"Yes, I will take a teaspoon of sugar as well."

"Here is a lump of sugar. I could not find a spoon, but I did find a chopstick."

"How will I stir my tea with a chopstick, Marybeth?"

Marybeth and Jackson laughed.

The Seed

Mr. Johnson walks around his farm. He checks to make sure his scarecrow is still standing. He made that scarecrow from an old corn sack. He walks by a pigpen. He sees a rabbit that snuck into the pigpen from the barnyard.

Then he spots a seed that is on top of the soil. He wonders if it will ever sprout. He has a daydream that the seed sprouts into a beanstalk. A firefly zips by and shatters his daydream. Then his eye follows the firefly to the farmhouse. There is a rainbow over the farmhouse! What a beautiful sight!

Grayson's First Day

Grayson is a freshman at a college in the southwest. Today Grayson meets his roommate. Their room has a skylight! Grayson cannot wait for school to start.

First he must go to the bookstore to buy eight textbooks. His textbooks cost a lot of money.

When he gets back to his room, he sees a note stuck to the corkboard. *Grayson, meet me at the football game!*

When Grayson gets to the football game, the team has made a touchdown! Someone snaps a photo of him as he cheers.

"Maybe that will be in the yearbook," he thinks.

Bob and Sam's Rainy Hike

Wind whips over the path. Rain falls in buckets. The rain turns the sunny day as dark as night. Bob and Sam were hiking when the storm began.

"I can't see!" Bob shouts. "I didn't bring a flashlight!"

"We didn't know it would storm!" Sam calls back. "I hope it'll clear up soon."

"I don't see the trail anymore!"

"I can't find the map, Bob!"

"We'll be soaked if we ever make it back to the car."

Boom! There is a clap of thunder and a flash of lightning. Sam and Bob probably won't go on a hike anytime soon.

Meg's Shoe

Meg and Kevin walk through a barn on a farm. Meg stops.

"I can't move," she says. "My shoe is stuck in this plank! It won't budge!"

"I'll get a crowbar. Maybe that'll help, Meg."

"I knew I shouldn't have worn these shoes on a farm."

Kevin asks the farmer for a crowbar. Then he tries to pry out her shoe. The shoe flies across the barn and lands in a sheep pen. One sheep starts to chew on her red shoe.

"I won't lie to you, Meg. I think that you'll need to get a new pair of shoes."

Party Time

"What time does the party start?" Mom asks.

"I'm meeting Fred at eight o'clock. We will help set up."

People on our street hold a party each year. It's a celebration for summer.

"I'll see you at the party," Mom says. "I'm going to make dip before I go."

"Fred's bringing chips. They'll go well with that dip."

"Who's bringing watermelon?"

"Albert. He's growing a few in his garden patch close to the woods."

"Is Ling bringing hot dogs? She's a grilling champ!"

"I think so. I'm getting hungry, Mom. This party'll be fun!"

Lost

Jim's late for a meeting. He can't find any street signs. A girl sitting on a stoop looks at him.

"I think he's lost," she says to her dog.

Jim looks at his map. He walks down several streets but gets even more lost. He sees a farmer on a tractor.

Jim asks, "Which way is Pine Street? I'm very lost."

"It's right here." The farmer points out Pine Street on the map.

Jim walks back to Pine Street. He spots a girl sitting on a stoop talking to her dog.

"Haven't I been on this street before?" he thinks.

Water Bubbles

I overhear a few men talking.

"Didn't you hear? Some strange things are going on at Lake Fishland."

Lake Fishland is a huge body of water near town.

"What's going on?"

"Huge bubbles are floating up in the center of Lake Fishland. My dad said it's a monster."

"I don't believe it!"

"Why wasn't it on the news?"

"It'll be on the news tonight."

Gossip spreads all over town. Everyone is talking about such strange bubbling. I'm not sure what to think.

Then I watch the news. There's a small volcano under the water! That's what has been bubbling!

The Secret Room

Tom had a tree in his yard. He cut it down. His friend Pam came to visit.

"Look, Tom. I haven't seen that round window before!"

"I'm guessing the tree was blocking it. I didn't know it was there."

"It looks like it's in the attic. We'll find it!" Pam said.

Tom and Pam run up to his attic.

"I don't see the round window, Tom. Shouldn't it be on this side of the house?"

"I can't find it."

"What's this?" Pam pokes a hole in the wall. A brick falls out.

"It's a secret room, Pam! There's that round window!"

Tough Decisions

"I love looking at paint chips!" shouted Mom. She brought me along with her to the paint store. She wanted to paint our kitchen a new color. We have been walking around this store *forever*. I could have climbed a mountain in the time we have been at this store.

Mom has changed her mind so many times. First Mom liked the bright colors, but now she's leaning towards the pale shades. A salesperson asked us if we needed help. Mom picked up a paint chip.

"No, this is it!" she smiled.

"Mom," I asked, "isn't that the same color that our kitchen is painted now?"

At Practice

My reading teacher is also the track coach. Each day at practice, he makes us run drills. We practice jumping and throwing. Ash jumps over the hurdles. Jake does a long jump. He is the best jumper on the team. Once he jumped eight feet! Jake can also throw the farthest.

At practice we often run races. I raced my friend Cho last week, but I lost to her. Coach said that the race looked close. Cho only beat me by a few paces. Next week, we will race again. Ash has been helping me practice. I am dreaming of winning!

A Trip to the Zoo

My class went to the zoo. We saw lots of animals. I liked seeing gorillas that were running and spinning around their cage. They even hugged each other!

In the fish tanks, I saw tons of fish swimming. I liked the spotted fish. One fish rubbed up against the side of the tank. Maybe it had an itch.

In the rabbit cage, some rabbits were hopping and jumping all over the place. They looked like they might want to be petted.

In the reptile hut, Rob yelled, "Jane, you're stepping on a snake!" Jane screamed.

Then Rob yelled, "Just kidding!" I didn't think it was funny.

Water, Water, Everywhere

"I can't take this any longer!" roared my sister, running her hands through her hair. Water had been dripping from the ceiling all day long. We jammed a bucket under the drip. Now that bucket was nearly full, and water was still plopping down. The annoying sound showed no sign of stopping!

"Did you talk to the plumber?" I asked my sister. She nodded.

Just then Dad plodded in, after a long day of digging our new garden.

"Did you see a red bucket, kids? I need it to water the plants," he said. Then he tripped over the bucket and water spilled everywhere.

"I think you found it," I said.

The School Play

"There are more clothes here than I have ever seen!" Fran declared. Fran and Beth rooted through a costume closet. They had to pick out costumes for the school play.

"It looks like this was knitted by hand," Beth exclaimed, reaching up to the top rack and pulling down a blue sweater.

Fran rubbed a silk tie between her hands. "This feels so soft!" she said, setting it on the growing pile of clothes they had picked out. "Do you think the cop character could use this shirt in the show?"

"It looks like the perfect shirt, Fran!"

"I can tell this will be a good show!"

Lost

"That leaning tree looks familiar. I think we walked by it before!" Taj shouted.

Mike stepped over a fallen branch. "Didn't we bring anything to help us find our way back? A flashlight? A map?" he asked.

"No."

Taj and Mike were lost in the forest. They had been hiking when the daylight began creeping away. The sun was now setting, and they couldn't find their way home. Leaves crunched under their feet as they walked around. They were feeling hopeless.

Then a light blinked nearby. Mike's mom came running towards them carrying a flashlight.

"I have been looking all over for you both!" she said. She hugged them.

Ron Unplugged

Caitlin made a mix CD of music for her friend Ron. She recalled that he liked many types of music. His favorite refrain was from a song by The Reruns called "Unlock My Heart." The Reruns were a band that remade old songs. They rewrote the music to make a remix.

Caitlin called the CD *Ron Unplugged.* She wrapped it for his birthday. How would Ron react to this gift?

Ron unknotted the bow and unwrapped the box. His glowing eyes showed that he loved the gift, but he didn't know how to react.

"Caitlin," he cried, "this is the most thoughtful gift ever!"

The Tent

These directions are very unclear. First I must unwrap the box. Then I must unknot the strings. Then I should retie them another way. After that I must unfold the tent and unsnap all the snaps.

I'm going to refrain from yelling at this tent! I must remain calm if I am going to get this tent up before night falls. This tent cannot be unsafe to use!

Now I must unroll the flaps. This thing is impossible! Who knew that putting up a tent would be this tough? Someone should rewrite those directions. I don't think I'll ever recover from this camping experience.

Overdue

"Dear, that book is overdue. This is the third time you returned a book late," said Mr. Biblo, a librarian.

"Mr. Biblo, I just enjoyed that book so much. I could not put it down," gushed Jen. "I was overjoyed at how it ended. I never would have predicted *that* ending."

"Yes, dear, but you should prepare better next time. Because your book is late, I didn't have enough time to presort the shelving carts."

"I'm sorry, Mr. Biblo. Can I do anything to make up for it?"

"Well, that garden out front is overgrown. If you pick a few weeds, I'll overlook your late fine just this once."

Dinner for Grandma

Dear Ray,

I am so glad you'll prepare a birthday dinner for Grandma. Here are a few tips for cooking a meal.

- Put all the ingredients near your workspace. You can even prewash and precut the vegetables.
- Do not overbeat the eggs. They will get too stiff.
- Be sure to preheat the oven before cooking. The meat should not be overdone.
- Do not overuse any spices. Too much pepper will make Grandma sneeze.
- Clear gunk out of the drain or the sink will overflow!

I wish I could help you prepare dinner, though I know your cooking will be great.

Best,
Wendy

Mel's Stolen Earrings

"I'll preside over this case," Sue the cop told Mel. "What did the thief take?"

"He took my favorite earrings. They go well with my black dress. I don't know how he broke in."

"Do you recall what the thief looked like?"

"No. He jumped out that window into the unlit alley."

Sue wrote *suspect unknown* in her notebook. She would work overtime in order for justice to prevail. She asked Mel a few more questions. She didn't want to overlook any detail.

"Relock your doors, Mel," Sue reminded her.

That night, Mel received a call.

"We found the thief!" Sue said. "I will return your earrings soon."

Costume Ball

Last week my school threw a costume ball. The planning committee worked overtime to prepare our gym in time for the ball. They redecorated the gym with lights and streamers. It looked unlike any gym I had ever seen. I did think that those disco lights were overkill, though.

Before the dance I predicted what each of my pals would dress as. A few pals bought premade costumes, while some reused old clothes to make a new outfit. At the end of the night, we all unmasked ourselves. We called it "The Great Unveiling."

Overall I can report that my pals and I had a fun time at the ball.

My Dead Plant

I have been incredibly busy this week due to my employment at the Snack Shack. When my alarm rudely woke me up this morning, I saw that the plant I kept next to my window had died. A few leaves were badly crushed.

Instantly, I thought our cat had snacked on my plant.

"That cat has been outside all week," my dad said. My mom nodded sternly in agreement.

To my embarrassment, my dad told me no one had touched my plant. "You clearly forgot to water it," he said.

To my amazement, my plant quickly came back to life. It had not died! I now water my plant daily.

The Town Meeting

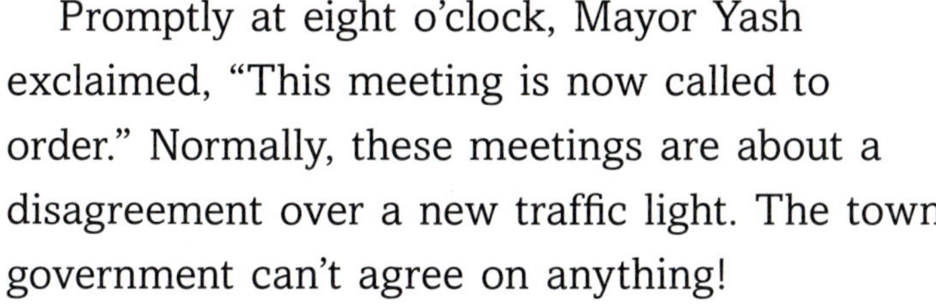

Promptly at eight o'clock, Mayor Yash exclaimed, "This meeting is now called to order." Normally, these meetings are about a disagreement over a new traffic light. The town government can't agree on anything!

"I need help," Yash said calmly. "There is not enough involvement in the town picnic. I need commitment from people. This Friday we will be getting a hot dog shipment and there is no one to cook them."

A man shyly raised his hand. "I'll bring a grill to our town square."

"My band will gladly provide music!" a girl kindly suggested.

Soon, everyone had volunteered to help with something. There would be a picnic after all!

Spring Cleaning

Yesterday Mom was in her cleaning mode. She told me to be helpful and clean my room.

As I trudged up the stairs, she yelled, "Make your room spotless! Don't let me catch you playing a game instead!"

Cleaning my room is an endless task. I have too much stuff. It is useless to try to shove another thing in my closet. I must be careful when I open it.

While Mom swept the kitchen with a powerful vacuum, I snuck outside to pick a few flowers.

When Mom saw them in a vase on the table, she said, "How thoughtful! You still must clean your room!"

A New Puppy

Chad and Ruth go to a city animal shelter. They are hopeful they will find a dog to take home.

First they see a dog with golden fur that barks loudly. "I don't think we'll get a restful sleep with his yapping," Chad jokes.

"We would have many sleepless nights," agrees Ruth.

Next they see a black dog with huge teeth. "His bite would be painful," exclaims Ruth. "I don't want him to take a mouthful of my arm."

"Turn around, Ruth! Look at that brown puppy. He looks harmless. The white spot on his ear is cute!"

"We'll take him!"

Chad and Ruth are grateful they found the puppy.

The Camp Klutz

"How did you get that dreadful cut?" the nurse kindly asked me on my third trip to the camp infirmary that summer.

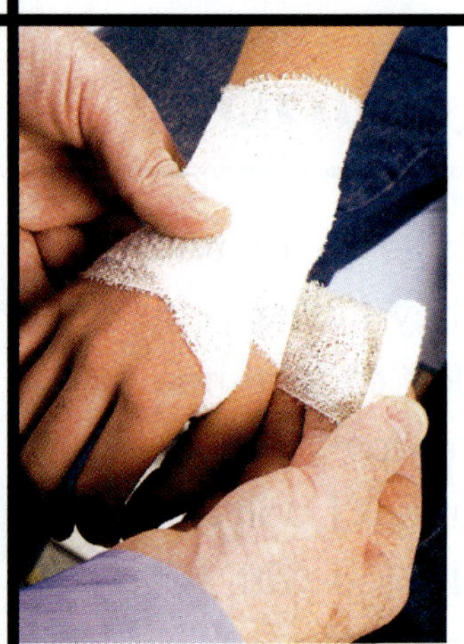

"I tripped over some sports equipment that was on the baseball field," I replied calmly.

"Needless to say, you should be more careful around camp."

The nurse put some ointment on my cut. It stung badly! That ointment was nearly more painful than the cut itself. I thanked her for the bandage and gladly left.

As I skipped briskly down the wooden stairs, I tripped and landed flat on my face.

To my embarrassment, a bunch of other campers saw my fall. I am a hopeless klutz.

Rose's Necklace

"Wasn't that the same thing that your dream was about?" asked Troy bluntly.

"Yes!" Rose shouted. They watched the news in amazement. There was a segment on jewels that everyone thought were fake and worthless. They turned out to be real.

A few sleepless nights ago, Rose had a dream that a necklace her grandma gave her was made of real diamonds.

Just then, their dad walked in the room. He looked hopeful. He quickly asked Rose, "Where is that necklace your grandma gave you?"

"He's thinking that it is real!" snickered Troy.

"Dad," Rose said grimly, "that's just wishful thinking."

"Or is it?" their dad replied slyly.

A Day at the Beach

When I was at the seashore last weekend, I saw a pair of seagulls flying high in the sky. The two birds landed on the beach near my pal Tad. I am glad my friend came with me!

First, we splashed around in the cold ocean. The cool sea felt good. Then, I took a quick nap while Tad dug a hole in the sand. I needed that rest! When I woke up, the warm sun was shining down on the hot sand.

"Look over there!" shouted Tad.

I saw a big ship out in the sea. "That boat is huge!" I yelled back. I wondered where it was going.

Bedtime Stories

My father tells great stories. I enjoy hearing the tales he recites. I love when my dad talks like the characters.

Once he spoke like a bug stuck under a rock. He kept talking like a bug until I said, "Dad, insects don't talk even if they are trapped beneath a stone!"

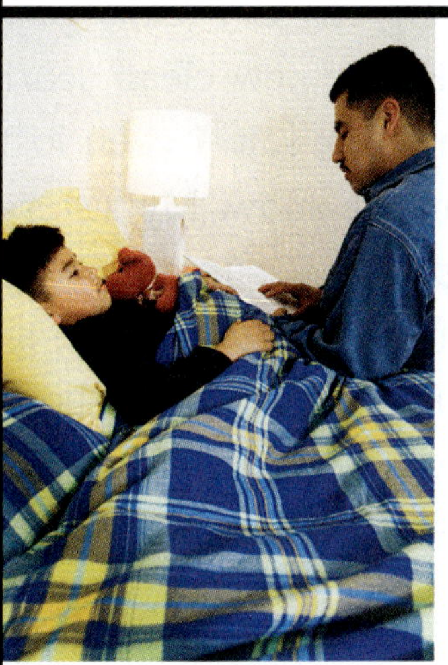

Another time my dad told a tale about an airplane with too many seats. This jet had to eject a few chairs while in flight. I don't think it was a true story.

When a story is over, my dad turns off my bedroom light. When the lamp is switched off, I know it is the end.

Winter and Summer

Winter started early this year. It feels like just yesterday that the hot breezes of late summer were here. Now cold winter gusts are blowing. Today it stopped raining and started snowing. My dry jeans got wet when I went outside. My new clean scarf is now dirty from the rock salt. I even lost an old white glove in the snow. My sister found it this morning.

I hope that this winter will be short, but all the weather reports say it will be long. Even though winter makes me sad, I know that I will be happy again in the summer. I hate winter, but I like summer.

Grandma's Tree

Liz looked at the tree in her backyard. As a young girl, her grandma had planted a small sapling there. Now, her grandma was an old woman and that sapling had grown into a huge tree. Though she lived far away, Liz felt close to her grandma whenever she sat under the tree or stood next to the swing her mom had tied over a branch.

A few flowers grew beneath the tree. Many bugs zipped above those flowers. Liz was sad that her grandma could not be here to be a part of her backyard fun. She was very glad her grandma had planted that tree.

May Hears a Noise

"What was that deafening sound?" cried May.

"I didn't hear any loud noise, only a soft thud," said Brad.

"It woke me up!"

"May, that clunk wasn't any louder than a whisper."

"It sounded like a scream! It came from upstairs."

"I'll take a quick look in the attic," Brad said. "Stay here."

"No! I'd rather go with you to take a fast peek, Brad."

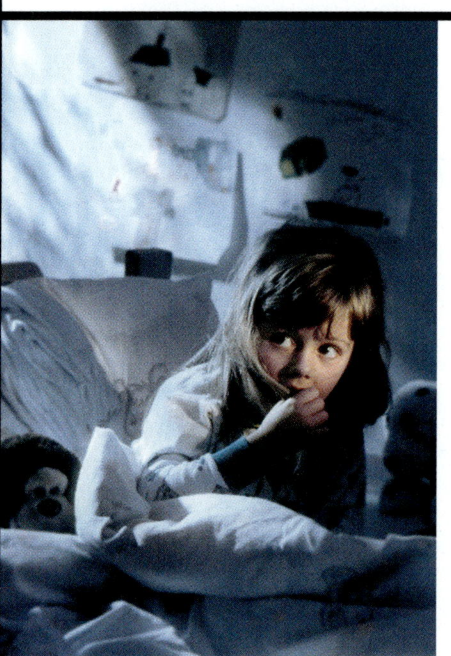

May and Brad climbed swiftly up the stairs into the attic. They saw a window shutter swaying quickly in the wind. It swung open and shut with a bang. May slowly pulled it back from the wall while Brad pushed the lock shut.

"Problem solved!" May exclaimed.

Hot and Cold

Dave and Eve were playing "Hot and Cold." Dave hid a toy boat behind a red bucket near their playroom. When Eve walked far from the pail, Dave yelled "cold." When she stepped close to the bucket, Dave shouted "hot."

Once Eve found the toy ship, she told Dave, "We need to find more people to play our awesome game!"

They saw a sad child in front of his house. He was hard at work weeding the garden.

Dave and Eve asked, "Would you like to play 'Hot and Cold' with us?"

"Yes!" said the kid. His face lit up brightly. He was very glad to be invited to play.

The Show

"It's my pleasure to present the star of our show!"

A woman with a kind face rose up from a seat on stage. She began to sing. A bright light shone on the stage, gleaming off a sparkling ring on her hand. Her voice seemed to ring out into the concert hall.

"Next our star will show you a brave kind of trick!"

A rope dropped down. The woman took hold of it and flew into the air as if she were light as a feather. When she landed back on stage, she turned to face the crowd. Everyone clapped for her. Someone threw a single rose to her.

What Should We Do?

"We always do the same thing. Let's try something new!" Ted exclaims.

Peg snaps a rubber band while she thinks. "We could see that rock band play at the fair."

"Or we could sit by a river bank and skim a rock or two across."

"We could take our coins to the bank or buy a new kitchen fan."

"Or we could see that play that just opened. I'm such a theater fan, Peg."

"This isn't fair, Ted. We have too many choices!"

"We'll just do it all. We have the rest of this weekend."

"I'm going to need a rest after so much fun."

Ted does up the snaps on his jacket. "Let's go!"

Painting

Last year as Jan ate a roll with some jam, she decided to paint her kitchen.

She patted her chin to brush off some crumbs. Then she used a roll of tape to protect her floor. She stirred the paint in the can with a stick. She thought, "I can do this!"

When she finished painting, Jan looked at her kitchen. It was a mess.

"Where did I stick that soap?" she wondered. She didn't want dried flakes to jam her drain.

As she washed a paint brush in her sink, a can fell over. The paint began to sink into the carpet.

"I'll never get this out!" she cried.

Coco

Greg picked up a pen and wrote a story. It was a school report about his pet. He has a dog named Coco.

Coco has brown spots on her ear. She has a small scratch on her nose. Her favorite food is peanut butter. Greg taught Coco some tricks.

Coco likes to scratch at tree bark. When she spots a squirrel in the yard, Coco will bark. The squirrel tricks Coco into running into the fence.

When Greg goes to school each day, Coco makes a sad, droopy face. Greg must pet her before he can leave. At night Coco stays in a pen.

Greg and Coco are best pals.

Cole and Gail's Robot

Cole and Gail make a plan to build a robot for the school science fair. This is their plan:

Aug. – Sketch a design.

Sept. – Sign up for a spot at the fair.

Oct. – Make a list of parts we need.

Nov. – Save up enough money to buy parts.

Dec. – Buy the robot parts from a store.

Jan. – Put together the body.

Feb. – Put together the arms and legs.

Mar. – Do a test to make sure the robot moves.

Apr. – Make a poster explaining the robot.

May – Present our robot at the fair.

June – Find out if we won!

"That is a lot to do," said Cole. "We should get started!"

Greg's List

"I got nothing done yesterday!" cried Greg. "This week I'm going to organize my life." He made a list:

> *Mon. – Go to the grocery store. Buy some food.*
>
> *Tues. – Visit Grandpa. Show him photos from my trip.*
>
> *Wed. – Go to the library. Check out a book on frogs.*
>
> *Thurs. – Write a report on frogs for school.*
>
> *Fri. – See a film with Zane and Jean.*
>
> *Sat. – Eat dinner with my family.*
>
> *Sun. – Go to the town picnic at Fisher Park.*

At the end of the week, Greg looked at his list.

"Wow," he thought. "I did each thing on this list. I'm going to make a list for next week, too!"

Will's Appointment

Will cannot bend his left arm. He has an appointment with Dr. Martin.

His dad wrote him a note with directions to the office. Will has a hard time reading the note. He strains his eyes to read the sloppy note.

Take Main St. to First Ave. Turn right at the light. Follow Penny Ln. to the end. Make a left on King Blvd. Go past the Expressway exit ramp. You will see Mr. and Mrs. Shaw's shop on your right. The office of Dr. Martin is on the third floor of that building.

As Will waits to see Dr. Martin, he hopes that he will feel better soon.

The Letter

"Yes, sir!" shouts Rick to Gen. Brown. Rick is in charge of delivering a very important letter from Gen. Brown to Sen. Jones. Gen. Brown had sketched a few notes to show Rick where to go.

Follow Hilldale Hwy. to Gray St.

Make a left onto Silver Dr.

Turn right on Park Pl.

Make a quick right on Thorn Rd.

You will see a tall white condo at the end of Thorn Rd.

Sen. Jones lives in Apt. 3.

Rick hands the letter to Sen. Jones. He waits for a reply.

After a short time, Sen. Jones says, "Tell him everything seems fine."

Travel Advice

Dear Prof. Conway,

I hear you're going to Mt. Wild on Sat. I went there last Aug. It was hot, but the weather is great in Sept. and Oct. Mr. and Mrs. Clark will be going there on Sun. or Mon. Maybe you will see them!

When you drive there, avoid Swift Ave. A crew has been repairing the road since last Apr. I think the construction will be done in Dec.

If you have time, drive down Music Ln. to see Lake Blue. Tues. is the best day to rent a boat. The lake gets too crowded on Wed. and Thurs. Have a nice trip!

Best,
Ms. Brooks

I Can't Stand It!

Dear Rep. Preston,

Last Fri., my family moved into a house on Spruce St. It is a pleasant neighborhood. I like that row of trees over on Pine Rd. Our neighbors, Mr. and Dr. Swain, brought a pie on Sat. They asked us to join them for supper on Sun.

All was well until Mon. morning when a loud sound shook the floors. I learned that the city is digging a tunnel under our house! The drilling is very noisy. I hear that it will last until next Jan. Please tell the workers not to start at six in the morning. I can't stand it anymore!

Many thanks,
Mr. Tweed

Decodable Scope and Sequence

All decodable reading passages include 75% previously taught sound spellings and from 15% to 20% previously taught high frequency words.

	LESSON	SOUND SPELLINGS	HIGH FREQUENCY WORDS	PASSAGE TITLES
UNIT 1 • CHAPTER 1	1	Letter/Sound correspondence: *s, m, a* (short), *t*	a, and, for, the, said	1. Sam's Mat 2. In the Ring
	2	Letter/Sound correspondence: *h, p, i* (short), *n*	make, no, me, I, come	1. The Hat 2. Min in the Pit
	3	Review lessons 1 and 2	was, into, do, saw, with	1. The Shop 2. Ham in a Pan
	4	Letter/Sound correspondence: *d, o* (short), *b, c* (/s/ and /k/)	she, he, are, look, to	1. The Cod 2. Dinner for Doc and Dan
	5	Letter/Sound correspondence: *ck, r, u* (short), *g* (/g/ and /j/)	where, we, find, go, you	1. The Pug Dog 2. Huck and the Tick
	6	Review lessons 4 and 5	away, be, see, my, came	1. Rock in My Sock 2. Rob's Rug
UNIT 1 • CHAPTER 2	1	Letter/Sound correspondence: *j, f, e* (short), *l*	two, play, blue, jump, little	1. Jen and Fin 2. Jim the Duck
	2	Letter/Sound correspondence: *z, ch, w, k*	one, down, funny, help, three	1. One Funny Dog 2. Help Zeb
	3	Review lessons 1 and 2	yellow, here, all, ate, black	1. The Big, Fat Bug 2. Ken and Fez
	4	Letter/Sound correspondence: *qu, y, x, v*	four, good, have, like, must	1. A Box to Fix the Van 2. The Quiz
	5	Letter/Sound correspondence: *wh, ng, sh, th* (/th/ and /TH/)	old, new, now, take, of	1. Songs 2. New Fish
	6	Review lessons 4 and 5	our, brown, eat, out, please	1. Beth's Pals 2. The Shack
UNIT 1 • CHAPTER 3	1	Short vowel *a* word families: *–ag, –an, –amp, –ack* Blends: *st, pl, cr, sc*	pretty, ride, so, soon, that	1. What's Inside? 2. Going Camping
	2	Short vowel *i* word families: *–ift, –ip, –ill, –ig* Blends: *dr, sl, tw, sw*	there, this, how, under, they	1. How Will They Get Back? 2. Drill and Fill
	3	Review lessons 1 and 2	well, too, white, will, yes	1. Stan Is Not Well 2. Pip Zips
	4	Short vowel *o* word families: *–op, –ock, –ot, –ond* Blends: *cl, bl, pr, fl*	say, want, after, ask, fly	1. At the Pond 2. Time for Bed
	5	Short vowel *u* and *e* word families: *–un, –ust, –ent, –ell* Blends: *sp, tr, sm, cr*	went, from, give, her, when	1. The Rent 2. The Tents
	6	Review lessons 4 and 5	some, think, giving, just, open	1. The Gift 2. The Well

LESSON	SOUND SPELLINGS	HIGH FREQUENCY WORDS	PASSAGE TITLES
UNIT 2 • CHAPTER 1			
1	Long vowels: *a, a_e, ay, o, o_e, oa*	before, stop, walk, live, what	1. A Trip to the Store 2. The Red Oak
2	Long vowels: *i_e, ie, u, ue, e, ea*	over, thank, them, who, may	1. We Like to Read 2. Camping
3	Review lessons 1 and 2	put, round, again, around, gave	1. On the Farm 2. Gale's Birthday
4	*r*–controlled vowels: *ar, air, are, eer, ear*	tell, goes, best, any, green	1. The Race 2. The Dare
5	*r*–controlled vowels: *ur, ir, er, or, oar, oor*	these, by, both, made, those	1. Yuri's Spurs 2. Poor Kirk
6	Review lessons 4 and 5	call, cold, could, use, or	1. A Fun Jar 2. The Storm
UNIT 2 • CHAPTER 2			
1	Vowel digraphs: *ew, oo, ui, ie* Blends: *br, st, thr, shr*	pull, every, wash, fast, read	1. The List 2. On a Cruise
2	Vowel digraphs: *aw, au, ei, ea* Blends: *str, tr, squ, spr*	why, five, sing, wish, know	1. The Kite 2. Maud's Claw
3	Review lessons 1 and 2	found, sleep, work, better, once	1. Paul 2. Claud the Thief
4	Long vowel word families: *–ail, –ate, –oe, –ow,* *–ute,–ue* Blends: *sn, bl, gr, gl*	done, fall, hold, then, bring	1. The Snow 2. The Date
5	Long vowel word families: *–y,– ild,– ite, –ight, –ey,* *–eech* Blends *sk, fr, scr*	draw, far, were, hurt, light	1. Fred and the Bear 2. What Will You Draw?
6	Review lessons 4 and 5	carry, drink, always, full, keep	1. Skip and Joe 2. Wish on a Star
UNIT 2 • CHAPTER 3			
1	Syllables: differentiate between 1- and 2-syllable words	long, clean, grow, kind, because	1. The Flower Garden 2. Pop's Big Day
2	Syllables: 2-syllable regular and nonsense words	much, ball, myself, shall, been	1. The Spaceship 2. The Spaceman
3	Review lessons 1 and 2	together, never, show, try, bear	1. The Hike 2. The Campers
4	Divide words into syllables	boy, only, would, warm, bell	1. To a Parade 2. The Surprise
5	Divide words into syllables	bread, own, small, apple, their	1. Lunchtime! 2. My Buddy
6	Review lessons 4 and 5	bird, brother, pick, start, baby	1. Sounds from a Bush 2. The Big Game

LESSON	SOUNDS SPELLINGS	HIGH FREQUENCY WORDS	PASSAGE TITLES
1	Complex consonant patterns: *ph, wr, nch, tch*	seven, cake, birthday, your, today	1. Your Birthday 2. A Weird Day
2	Complex consonant patterns: *dge, sch, nce, nge*	back, boat, car, its, chair	1. A Twinge for Fudge 2. At the Winter Ball
3	Review lessons 1 and 2	day, farm, write, flower, ground	1. The Dry Farm 2. Phil's Tale
4	Diphthongs: *oi, oy*	chicken, upon, doll, father, game	1. A Chicken That Oinks 2. A Game of Royals
5	Diphthongs: *ou, ow*	buy, hand, children, door, feet	1. A Monster House 2. A Crowd of Clouds
6	Review lessons 4 and 5	garden, head, many, coat, duck	1. Captain Oily Oyster 2. Pigs in the Garden

UNIT 3 • CHAPTER 1

LESSON	SOUNDS SPELLINGS	HIGH FREQUENCY WORDS	PASSAGE TITLES
1	Silent letters: *h, gn*	fire, girl, off, hill, corn	1. Fresh Corn 2. Sara the Designer
2	Silent letters: *kn, mb*	egg, does, fish, goodbye, home	1. Did You Know? 2. Ned the Knight
3	Review lessons 1 and 2	cow, eye, very, floor, grass	1. The Sick Lamb 2. Cooking with Dad
4	Complex vowel pattern: *ou* (bought, couple, soup)	horse, wood, don't, squirrel, house	1. A Squirrel in the House 2. Doug the Cowboy
5	Complex vowel patterns: *al* (fall), *eigh* (weigh), *ol* (cold), *wa* (wash)	morning, paper, which, ring, song	1. Gold Bars 2. The Sleigh Ride
6	Review lessons 4 and 5	kitty, first, mother, stick, robin	1. Signs of the Seasons 2. Mother's Birthday

UNIT 3 • CHAPTER 2

LESSON	MORPHOLOGY SKILL	HIGH FREQUENCY WORDS	PASSAGE TITLES
1	Compound words	snow, about, letter, name, right	1. The Letter 2. Snowflakes
2	Compound words	picture, sister, milk, nest, laugh	1. My Sister's Notebook 2. Would You Like Some Tea?
3	Review lessons 1 and 2	rabbit, eight, seed, money, school	1. The Seed 2. Grayson's First Day
4	Contractions with *not* and *will*	wind, night, rain, sheep, shoe	1. Rob and Sam's Rainy Hike 2. Meg's Shoe
5	Contractions with *is* and *am*	party, way, street, close, farmer	1. Party Time 2. Lost
6	Review lessons 4 and 5	water, didn't, body, window, friend	1. Water Bubbles 2. The Secret Room

UNIT 3 • CHAPTER 3

	LESSON	MORPHOLOGY SKILL	HIGH FREQUENCY WORDS	PASSAGE TITLES
UNIT 4 • CHAPTER 1	1	Inflected verb endings: –ed, –ing, –s	along, love, teacher, color, also	1. Tough Decisions 2. At Practice
	2	Consonant doubling with –ed and –ing	longer, talk, class, might, animal	1. A Trip to the Zoo 2. Water, Water, Everywhere
	3	Review lessons 1 and 2	clothes, more, than, couldn't, anything	1. The School Play 2. Lost
	4	Prefixes: un–, re–	most, thing, cried, music, another	1. Ron Unplugged 2. The Tent
	5	Prefixes: pre–, over–	book, near, third, dear, though	1. Overdue 2. Dinner for Grandma
	6	Review lessons 4 and 5	broke, took, dress, each, threw	1. Mel's Stolen Earrings 2. Costume Ball
UNIT 4 • CHAPTER 2	1	Suffixes: –ment and –ly	next, town, can't, o'clock, died	1. My Dead Plant 2. The Town Meeting
	2	Suffixes: –less and –ful	turn, order, catch, city, ear	1. Spring Cleaning 2. A New Puppy
	3	Review lessons 1 and 2	other, summer, dream, wasn't, he's	1. The Camp Klutz 2. Rose's Necklace
	4	Synonyms	high, pair, while, until, end	1. A Day at the Beach 2. Bedtime Stories
	5	Antonyms	part, tree, winter, hope, early	1. Winter and Summer 2. Grandma's Tree
	6	Review lessons 4 and 5	I'd, people, woke, face, I'll	1. May Hears a Noise 2. Hot and Cold
UNIT 4 • CHAPTER 3	1	Multiple–meaning words	I'm, such, present, same, woman	1. The Show 2. What Should We Do?
	2	Multiple–meaning words	kids, last, it's, year, fell	1. Painting 2. Out Trip to the Beach
	3	Review lessons 1 and 2	second, leave, wrote, food, happy	1. Baseball 2. Coco
	4	Abbreviations: months and days	should, yesterday, store, life, won	1. Cole and Gail's Robot 2. Greg's List
	5	Abbreviations: titles and addresses	left, seem, fine, hard, eyes	1. Will's Appointment 2. The Letter
	6	Review lessons 4 and 5	stand, family, hear, you're, going	1. Travel Advice 2. I Can't Stand It!

Acknowledgements

Photography

Page cover (top left): ©John W. Warden/Stock Connection Distribution/Alamy; cover (top right): ©Mariano Ruiz/Dreamstime.com; cover (bottom right): ©Viorika Prikhodko/iStockphoto; cover (bottom left): ©Corbis Royalty Free; iii: ©Polka Dot Images/Jupiter Images; iv: ©Herbert Cosby/Alamy; v: ©Corbis Royalty Free; vi: Photodisc/Getty Images Royalty Free; vii: ©Corbis Royalty Free; 2: ©Adriane Moll/zefa/Corbis; 3: ©Daniel Mirer/Corbis; 4: ©Masterfile Royalty Free; 5: ©Loungepark/Stone/Getty Images; 6: ©Catherine Karnow/CORBIS; 7: ©Herbert Cosby/Alamy; 8: ©SuperStock, Inc./SuperStock; 9: ©Index Stock Photography; 10: ©Romy Ragan/Alamy; 11: ©Visuals Unlimited/Corbis; 12: ©Brand X Pictures/Alamy; 13: ©Arco Images/Alamy; 14: ©Ragnar Schmuck/zefa/Corbis; 15: ©Image Source Pink/Getty Images Royalty Free; 16: ©Richard Hutchings/Corbis; 17: ©Getty Images Royalty Free; 18: ©Getty Images Royalty Free; 19: ©Janis Christie/PhotoDisc/Getty Images; 20: ©David Leahy/Digital Vision/Getty Images; 21: ©Sean Justice/Stone/Getty Images; 22: ©Adrian Sherratt/Alamy; 23: ©Corel Royalty Free; 24: ©Purestock/Getty Images; 25: ©Ana Maria Marques/Alamy; 26: ©Ragnar Schmuck/fStop/Getty Images; 27: ©David Young-Wolff/Photo Edit; 28: ©PhotoAlto/Milena Boniek/Getty Images; 29: ©Royalty Free/Corbis; 30: ©Bill Aron /Photo Edit; 31: ©Hans Reinhard/zefa/Corbis; 32: ©Comstock Royalty Free; 33: ©Bloomimage/Corbis; 34: ©Keith Leighton/Alamy; 35: ©Somos Images/Corbis; 36: ©Stockbyte/Getty Images Royalty Free; 37: ©David Davis Photoproductions/Alamy; 38: ©Jean Heguy/First Light/Getty Images; 39: ©Martin Ruegner/Digital Vision/Getty Images; 40: ©Thinkstock/Corbis; 41: ©Laura Ciapponi/Photonica/Getty Images; 42: ©Larry Allan/Bruce Coleman International; 43: ©O'Brien Productions/Corbis; 44: ©Royalty-Free/Corbis; 45: ©Corbis/Royalty Free; 46: ©Fernando Bueno/The Image Bank/Getty Images; 47: ©Digital Vision Ltd./SuperStock; 48: ©Design Pics Inc./Alamy; 49: ©Russ Merne/Alamy; 50: ©81a Productions/Photolibrary; 51: ©Royalty-Free/Corbis; 52: ©Image Shop/Corbis; 53: ©PhotoDisc/Getty Images Royalty Free; 54: ©PhotoDisc/Getty Images; 55: ©Aaron Cobbett/Stone/Getty Images; 56: ©Hans Strand/Jupiter Images; 57: ©Bee Ball/Riser/Getty Images; 58: ©SW Production/Jupiter Images; 59: ©Bloomimage/Corbis; 60: ©David Buffington/Blend Images/Getty Images; 61: ©P. Parviainen/Photo Researchers, Inc.; 62: ©Getty Images Royalty Free; 63: ©Eric Cahan/Corbis; 64: ©Niall McDiarmid/Alamy; 65: ©Pat Behnke/Alamy; 66: ©Ariel Skelley/CORBIS; 67: ©Royalty-Free/Corbis; 68: ©Gabe Palmer/Alamy; 69: ©PhotoDisc/Getty Images; 70: ©Royalty-Free/CORBIS; 71: ©Donald Miralle/Getty Images; 72: ©Andrew Tatnell/Alamy; 73: ©Ariel Skelley/CORBIS; Page 74: ©Beard & Howell/Digital Vision/Getty Images; 75: ©Paul Costello/Getty Images; 76: ©Digital Studios; 77: ©William Whitehurst/CORBIS; 78: ©Holt Studios International Ltd/Alamy; 79: ©Getty Images Royalty Free; 80: ©Image Source Pink/Image Source/Getty Images; 81: ©Bob Llewellyn/Jupiter Images; 82: ©Janusz Wrobel/Alamy; 83: ©Getty Images Royalty Free; 84: ©Dalgleish Images/Alamy; 85: ©Image Source/Fotosearch Royalty Free; 86: ©Corbis Royalty Free; 87: ©Hill Street Studios/Blend Images/Corbis; 88: ©Brian Mitchell/Alamy; 89: ©Getty Images Royalty Free; 90: ©DLILLC/Corbis; 91: ©JUPITERIMAGES/Thinkstock/Alamy; 92: ©Catherine Ledner/Stone/Getty Images; 93: ©Getty Images Royalty Free; 94: ©Louie Psihoyos/CORBIS; 95: ©mediacolor's/Alamy; 96: ©Rob Casey/Jupiter Images; 97: ©graficart.net/Alamy; 98: ©Corbis Royalty Free; 99: ©Caroline Woodham/Digital Vision/Getty Images; 100: ©Karl Grupe/Photonica/Getty Images; 101: ©Shaffer-Smith/Index Stock; 102: ©Tom Bean/CORBIS; 103: ©Donald Miralle/Taxi/Getty Images; 104: ©Photodisc/Getty Images Royalty Free; 105: ©José Fuste Raga/zefa/Corbis; 106: ©Carl & Ann Purcell/Jupiter Images; 107: ©Corbis/Royalty Free; 108: ©DEA/L.ROMANO/De Agostini Picture Library/Getty Images; 109: ©Bryan Eveleigh/Alamy; Page 110: ©Somos Images/Corbis; 111: ©Corbis Royalty Free; 112: ©Jeff Greenberg/The Image Works; 113: ©Dorling Kindersley/Getty Images; 114: ©Jupiter Images; 115: ©Education Photos/Alamy; 116: ©Bloomimage/Corbis; 117: ©Philip Lee Harvey/Taxi/Getty Images; 118: ©Thinkstock/Corbis; 119: ©Walter Hodges/Stone/Getty Images; 120: ©Benn Mitchell/Photographer's Choice/Getty Images; 121: ©Ryan McVay/Photodisc/Getty Images; 122: ©PhotosIndia.com LLC/Alamy; 123: ©Steve Warmowski/Jacksonville Journal-Courier/The Image Works; 124: ©Studio Paggy/IZA Stock/Getty Images; 125: ©Karl Kost/Alamy; 126: ©Bruce Miller/Alamy; 127: ©Andreas Pollok/Stone/Getty Images; 128: ©Getty Images Royalty Free; 129: ©ColorBlind Images/Blend Images/Corbis; 130: ©Image Source/Corbis; 131: ©LWA-Dann Tardif/CORBIS; 132: ©Gerhard Steiner/CORBIS; 133: ©Elizabeth Whiting & Associates/Alamy; 134: ©Lawrence Manning/Corbis; 135: ©rubberball/Getty Images; 136: ©Medioimages/Photodisc/Getty Images; 137: ©Eric Meola/Stone/Getty Images; 138: ©Kevin Cooley/Taxi/Getty Images; 139: ©Dale C. Spartas/CORBIS; 140: ©Jeff Greenberg/The Image Works; 141: ©Zigy Kaluzny/Stone/Getty Images; 142: ©Jack Hollingsworth/Corbis; 143: ©David Young-Wolff/Photo Edit; 144: ©altrendo images/Getty Images; 145: ©Royalty-Free/Corbis.